A GUIDE TO
MONASTIC GUEST HOUSES

J. Robert Beagle

*Dedicated with love
to the memory of
May Louise S. Regalbuto*

Cover design by Carole Masonberg
Cover illustration by Dhyann Samuelson
Page illustrations by Bob Griffiths

Morehouse-Barlow Co., Inc.
78 Danbury Road
Wilton, Connecticut 06897

Library of Congress Cataloging-in-Publication Data

Beagle, J. Robert.
 A guide to monastic guest houses / J. Robert Beagle.
 p. 000 cm.
 ISBN 0-8192-1445-0
 1. Monasteries—United States—Guest accommodations—Directories.
 I. Title.
 BX2505.B43   1989
 269' .6' 0973—dc19

Printed in the United States of America
by
BSC LITHO
Harrisburg, PA

Contents

Acknowledgments   ix
Preface   xi
Map . . . . xii, xiii

Arizona
Servants of Christ Monastery, Phoenix   1

Arkansas
The Abbey Retreat, Subiaco   3

California
Incarnation Priory, Berkeley   5
Mount Calvary Retreat House, Santa Barbara   7
Prince of Peace Abbey, Oceanside   9
St. Andrew's Priory, Valyermo   11
St. Paul Monastery, Palm Desert   13
The Retreat House, Big Sur   15
Woodside Priory, Portola Valley   17

Colorado
Holy Cross Abbey, Canon City   19
Monastery of St. Walburga, Boulder   21
St. Benedict's Monastery, Snowmass   23

Connecticut
Convent of St. Birgitta, Darien   25

District of Columbia
St. Anselm's Abbey, Washington   27

Georgia
Convent of St. Helena, Augusta   29
Monastery of the Visitation, Snellville   31

Illinois
Bethlehem House, Chicago 33

Indiana
St. Meinrad Archabbey Guest House, St. Meinrad 35

Iowa
Mississippi Abbey, Dubuque 37

Kentucky
Bethlehem Priory, Lexington 39
Gethsemani Abbey, Trappist 41

Maryland
All Saints Convent, Catonsville 43
Annunciation Monastery, Catonsville 45

Massachusetts
Emery House, West Newbury 47
Glastonbury Abbey, Hingham 49
Monastery of St. Mary and St. John, Cambridge . . 51
St. Benedict Priory, Still River 53
St. Joseph's Abbey Retreat House, Spencer 55
St. Scholastica Priory, Petersham 57

Michigan
St. Augustine's House, Oxford 59
St. Gregory's Abbey, Three Rivers 61

Missouri
Christina House Hermitages, Pevely 63
St. Louis Priory, St. Louis 65

Nebraska
Christ the King Priory, Schuyler 67

New Hampshire

The Common, Peterborough 69

New Jersey

St. Paul's Abbey, Newton 71

New Mexico

St. Michael's Forest Valley Priory, Tajique 73

New York

Abbey of the Genesee, Piffard 75
Convent of St. Helena, Vails Gate 77
Holy Cross Monastery, West Park 79
House of the Redeemer, New York City 81
Little Portion Friary, Mt. Sinai 83
Monastery of Mary the Queen, Elmira 85
Mount Saviour Monastery, Pine City 87
St. Cuthbert's House and
    St. Aidan's House, Brewster 89
St. Margaret's House, New Hartford 91
St. Mary's Convent, Peekskill 93
Transfiguration Monastery, Windsor 95

North Carolina

St. John's House, Durham 97
St. Luke's House, Lincolnton 99

Ohio

Convent of the Transfiguration, Cincinnati 101
Holy Protection Monastery, North Royalton 103

Oregon

Mount Angel Abbey Retreat House, St. Benedict . 105

Pennsylvania
Emmaus, Paoli 107
Orthodox Monastery of the Transfiguration,
   Ellwood City 109
St. Margaret's House, Philadelphia 111

Rhode Island
Portsmouth Abbey, Portsmouth 113

South Carolina
Holy Saviour Priory, Pineville 115

South Dakota
Blue Cloud Abbey, Marvin 117

Vermont
Weston Priory, Weston 119

Virginia
Monastery of the Visitation, Rockville 121

Washington
Convent of St. Helena, Seattle 123
St. Martin's Abbey Guest House, Lacey 125

Wisconsin
Convent of the Holy Nativity, Fond du Lac 127
De Koven Center, Racine 129
St. Norbert Abbey, De Pere 131

Acknowledgments

The completion of this guide required the assistance and cooperation of many persons, and I express my heartfelt gratitude to the monks and nuns, guest masters and guest sisters, who were so very kind and patient in providing the information needed. Moreover, my thanks to them for their many words of encouragement and expressions of prayerful support. May God reward them.

I extend particular appreciation to John Hinman, M.D. for his initial and continuing encouragement, to E. Allen Kelley, publisher, and to senior editor Deborah Grahame-Smith for her courteous and expert advice.

Preface

The custom of receiving guests in a monastery is as old as Christian monasticism itself. In the sixth century, St. Benedict (the founder of Western monasticism) observed in his Rule that "guests are never lacking in a monastery" and counseled his brethren to receive guests "as Christ himself." Many monasteries and convents are, in our time and in this spirit, open to those who seek a quieter place and a time of purposeful rest and reflection.

The monastic guest houses in this book represent a spectrum of Christian traditions, yet each extends a hearty welcome to all. Here are important points to remember:

- Arrange for your visit well in advance. Always address your request to the guest master or guest sister. Some monasteries close their guest house for brief periods of the year in the interest of community retreat, work, or rest. Others have become so popular that booking well in advance is not only advisable but necessary.

- As a guest, you will want to observe the monastery's particular customs and courtesies. In some, guests are lodged within the monastic enclosure; at others, in another building. So, too, customs vary as to where guests take their meals, the extent of their participation in church services, the parts of the monastery they may use, and the times of silence to be observed. The guest master or guest sister will familiarize you with the monastery's observances.

This book was not intended to be a guide to every monastic guest house nationwide. Rather, it is a compendium of responses received from selected monasteries. It is comprehensive but not complete. If the reader is led to "a place apart" where monastic hospitality is offered and a "holy leisure" is enjoyed, then this guide will have served its purpose.

Numbers here correspond to the page where the guest house entry appears in the guide. See Contents (page v).

SERVANTS OF CHRIST MONASTERY
6533 N. 39th Avenue
Phoenix, Arizona 85019

Telephone: (602) 841–8634.

Order: Servants of Christ (Episcopal).

Accommodations: Five guests (two women and three men) in single and twin rooms, two of which have private bath.

Meals: Three meals daily.

Charges: $40 per day for room and meals.

Directions: If driving, take I–17 (which becomes I–10 in Phoenix) to Bethany Home Road exit. Go west on Bethany Home Road to 39th Avenue and then north to the monastery.

If using public transportation, a Phoenix city bus stops in front of the monastery. Ask the guest master for information on specific bus number, etc.

History: This community of priests and. laymen was formed in 1968 to work among the poor.

Description: The monastery offers a place of quiet and refuge in the city of Phoenix.

Points of Interest: Scottsdale, Sun City, Sedona, and the Grand Canyon are all within easy access of Phoenix and the monastery.

THE ABBEY RETREAT
Coury House
Subiaco, Arkansas 72865

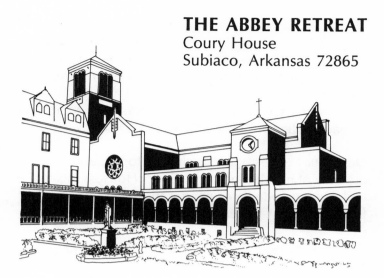

Telephone: (501) 934–4411.

Order: Benedictine monks (Roman Catholic).

Accommodations: Fifty guests in twenty-one twin-bedded rooms and four double-bedded rooms, each with private bath.

Meals: Three meals daily in the abbey guest dining room.

Charges: $30 per day for room and meals; $55 per weekend for an individual guest; and $90 per weekend for a couple.

Directions: By car, the abbey is 110 miles west of Little Rock on Highway 22 or 48 miles east of Fort Smith on Highway 22.
   By public transportation, take air transportation to Little Rock or Fort Smith; contact the guest master for further directions.

History: St. Benedict established a monastery at Subiaco, Italy, in the sixth century, and thirteen hundred years later, in 1878, New Subiaco was founded in the New World by monks from St. Meinrad's Abbey, Indiana. Early works included ministry to the German immigrant population and a school. Coury House was opened at New Subiaco Abbey in 1963 for those seeking "a place apart."

Description: The abbey, its church, tower, and cloisters are built of native sandstone. Coury House is located in a pleasant wooded area nearby and welcomes over two thousand guests a year.

Points of Interest: The majestic Mount Magazine is near the abbey.

Special Note: In addition to receiving individual guests for private retreats, Coury House offers preached retreats and directed retreats. A descriptive brochure is available from the abbey's guest master.

INCARNATION PRIORY
1601 Oxford Street
Berkeley, California 94709

Telephone: (415) 548–3406.

Orders: Order of the Holy Cross (Episcopal) and Benedictine monks (Roman Catholic).

Accommodations: Two guests in the monastery, each in single room and both with shared bath.

Meals: Evening meal only.

Directions: The guest master will provide directions on request.

Description: The Incarnation Priory is an ecumenical monastic house. It is the joint venture of the Episcopal Order of the Holy Cross and Roman Catholic Benedictine monks. Most of the monks work and study in the area during the day, returning to the priory for the evening meal at which guests may join them.

Points of Interest: The priory is close to the University of California at Berkeley and only thirty minutes from San Francisco.

MOUNT CALVARY RETREAT HOUSE
P.O. Box 1296
Santa Barbara, California 93102–1296

Telephone: (805) 962–9855.

Order: Order of the Holy Cross (Episcopal).

Accommodations: Thirty guests in fourteen single and nine twin rooms, all with shared bath.

Meals: Three meals daily.

Charges: $30 per person per day for room and meals.

Directions: If coming by car, request directions.
   If using public transportation, there is plane, train, and bus service to Santa Barbara. Arrange in advance to be met.

History: This house of the Order of the Holy Cross was established in 1947 by Fr. Karl Tiedemann, O.H.C. Mount Calvary was opened to serve as the order's retreat house and conference center on the West Coast.

Description: The retreat house was built in the style of a large Spanish house. It is dramatically situated on a ridge 1,250 feet above the city of Santa Barbara. Mount Calvary enjoys commanding views of the seacoast and the Pacific Ocean.

Special Note: Group retreats are given at Mount Calvary. Contact the guest master for a brochure and further information.

PRINCE OF PEACE ABBEY
Oceanside, California 92054

Telephone: (619) 430–1305 and 430–1306.

Order: Benedictine monks (Roman Catholic).

Accommodations: Twenty guests in the guest house, each in a twin-bedded room with private bath.

Meals: Three meals daily.

Charges: Suggested donation of $20 per person per day for room and meals.

Directions: By car, take I–5 to the city of Oceanside.
   If using public transportation, take bus or Amtrak train to Oceanside. Contact the guest master for further directions.

Description: The abbey, its monastery, church, and guest house are located about one hundred miles south of Los Angeles and thirty-five miles north of San Diego.

Points of Interest: The Mission San Luis Rey, dating from 1798, is near the abbey.

ST. ANDREW'S PRIORY

31001 N. Valyermo Road
P.O. Box 40
Valyermo, California 93563

Telephone: (805) 944–2178 or 944–2179.

Order: Benedictine monks (Roman Catholic).

Accommodations: Thirty-four guests in seventeen twin-bedded rooms in the guest house, each with private bath.

Meals: Three meals daily.

Charges: Suggested donation of $35 to $40 per day per person for room and meals.

Directions: By car from Los Angeles, take Route 14 to Pearblossom Highway exit. Go down Longview Road and then left onto Valyermo Road.
   By public transportation, take Greyhound to Palmdale or train to San Bernardino. Contact the guest master for further details.

History: St. Andrew's Abbey traces its roots to the Belgian Abbey of St. Andrew. Belgian monks were sent to China in 1929, and when expelled by the Communists in 1955, the community resettled in Valyermo. From the beginning, monastic hospitality has been a work of the monks here, and in 1965 a new guest house was opened.

Description: Valyermo is in the Mojave Desert just south of Los Angeles. The priory's buildings, contemporary in design, are set in a wooded area. The priory is known worldwide for its ceramics, and these are exhibited and sold at the Monastery Art and Gift Shop at the priory. Stations of the Way of the Cross are placed along the hillside here.

Special Note: The abbey sponsors workshops, group retreats, and days of recollection. Contact the priory's guest master for further information and literature.

ST. PAUL MONASTERY
44–660 San Pablo Avenue
Palm Desert, California 92260

Telephone: (619) 568–2200.

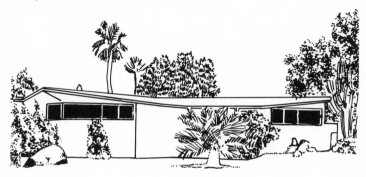

Order: Society of St. Paul (Episcopal).

Accommodations: Twenty guests (in two guest houses) in twin-bedded rooms, most with shared bath.

Meals: Three meals daily.

Charges: $30 per person per day for room and meals.

Directions: If driving, the monastery is north of Highway 111 in Palm Desert. When driving on I–10, take the Palm Desert exits.
  If using public transportation, the nearest airport is Palm Springs (twelve minutes away). There is bus service to Palm Springs, Palm Desert, and Indio. Air or bus arrivals will be met if prior arrangement is made.

History: This society of priests and brothers was founded in 1958 by Fr. Rene Bozarth. From its founding until 1976, the society had its monastery in Oregon. Now in

California, the society has a number of ministries: preaching, retreats, hospitality, and St. Paul's Press.

Description: The society has a 1½-acre plot of land in Palm Desert landscaped with tall cedar trees, cacti, ash, palms, and other desert growth suitable to the area's warm and dry climate. Completed in 1958, the monastery's eight buildings include Our Lady of the Desert Chapel, a library, a common building, and two guest houses. There are also a heated pool and spa.

Palm Desert is surrounded by mountains and desert. The Ariel Tram and Palm Springs are in the area.

Special Note: Contact the guest master for brochures and information about group retreats.

THE RETREAT HOUSE
Immaculate Heart Hermitage
Big Sur, California 93920

Telephone: (408) 667–2456.

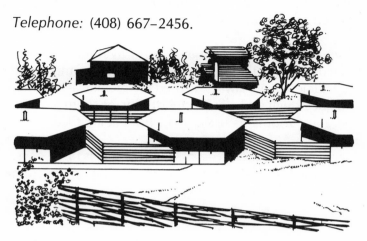

Order: Camaldolese monks (Roman Catholic).

Accommodations: Nine guests in the monastery and guest house, each in a single room with toilet and wash basin. Showers are shared.

Meals: Main meal (vegetarian) is delivered to guests in their rooms. Two other meals are available in the kitchen.

Charges: $25 per person per day for room and meals.

Directions: The hermitage is located at Lucia, off the Coast Highway (California Route 1), about twenty-five miles south of Big Sur and fifty-five miles south of Monterey. The hermitage entrance road, on the inland side of the highway, is marked by a large white cross.

If taking a plane or bus to Monterey, guests can be met (by prior arrangement) on Friday afternoons between 4:00 and 6:00 P.M.

History: The Camaldolese hermits are a reform within the Order of St. Benedict. Founded by St. Romuald near Arrezzo, Italy, in 1012, the hermits may lead both a solitary life and a life in community. New Camaldoli was opened at Big Sur in 1958.

Description: The hermitage is on a five-hundred-acre tract of land in the Santa Lucia mountain range. The Camaldolese have always favored the eremitical life-style, and guests will find every opportunity for solitude here. The guest rooms have views of the Pacific Ocean.

Special Note: A guest's usual length of stay is three days. Literature and further information may be gotten from the hermitage's guest master.

WOODSIDE PRIORY

302 Portola Road
Portola Valley, California 94025

Telephone: (415) 851–8220.

Order: Benedictine monks (Roman Catholic).

Accommodations: Ten guests in the guest house in single
and twin rooms, each with private bath.

Meals: Three meals daily.

Charges: Freewill donations accepted.

Directions: By car from San Francisco, take Route 280
South and exit at Alpine Road.
   By public transportation, take bus from San Francisco
to Portola Valley.

History: This Benedictine priory was founded in 1957.
Since its beginning, the monastery has had a school for
boys as well as a guest house for retreatants.

Description: The priory and guest house are in a beautiful, rustic area just south of San Francisco.

HOLY CROSS ABBEY

P.O. Box 351
Canon City, Colorado 81212

Telephone: (719) 275–8631.

Order: Benedictine monks (Roman Catholic).

Accommodations: Up to 123 guests in sixty-eight rooms (single and twin) in the guest house and Hedley House, all with shared baths.

Meals: Three meals daily.

Charges: Rooms are $14; breakfast is $3; lunch is $4; and dinner is $6.50. The total is $27.50 per person per day for room and three meals.

Directions: The abbey is located on U.S. Highway 50, two miles east of Canon City and thirty-eight miles west of Pueblo.

By public transportation, there is Greyhound bus service to Canon City.

History: Benedictine monks arrived in Colorado in 1886 and, after several moves, settled in Canon City in 1924. Just two years after the monks arrived in Canon City, the present monastery, chapel, and library were completed. Built of brick and granite, the handsome Gothic Revival buildings were placed on the National Register of Historic Places in 1983.

Description: The monastery, guest houses, and community center (with its gift shop) are on the more than two hundred acres owned by the abbey. Over half of this acreage is utilized as farmland.

Points of Interest: The Royal Gorge is in Canon City. Restored western towns and mines are here and in the neighboring town of Cripple Creek. In Colorado Springs are the U.S. Air Force Academy, the Space Control Center, and the beautifully landscaped Garden of the Gods.

Special Note: The abbey offers group retreats in addition to welcoming individual guests. Contact the abbey's guest master for further information.

MONASTERY OF ST. WALBURGA
6717 South Boulder Road
Boulder, Colorado 80303

Telephone: (303) 494–5733.

Order: Benedictine nuns
(Roman Catholic).

Accommodations: Up to
forty guests in the monastery and guest houses.
Rooms are single, twin,
triple, and one four-bedded
room. Some of the rooms
have private baths.

Meals: Three meals daily.

Charges: $26 to $28 per
person per day for room
and meals.

Directions: By car from Denver, take Highway 36 north,
exit at Table Mesa–South Boulder Road; go east on South
Boulder Road about two miles. Monastery will be on the
left.

If using public transportation, the "Louisville" bus from
Boulder will let you off in front of the monastery.

History: The Monastery of St. Walburga was begun in
the 1930s by nuns from the Abbey of St. Walburg in
Bavaria. The community now numbers about twenty
women, about half of whom are German. The nuns run
a small farm on which they raise cattle, chickens, and
llamas, and they produce artwork such as woven tapes-

21

tries, stained glass, liturgical vestments, and calligraphy.

Description: Guests are welcome to participate in the Divine Office, which is sung in its entirety daily. Some guests choose to work with the sisters in the house, garden, or farm as a way of sharing more fully in the monastic life.

Points of Interest: The Rocky Mountains.

Special Note: Contact the guest sister for information regarding group retreats.

ST. BENEDICT'S MONASTERY
1012 Monastery Road
Snowmass, Colorado 81654

Telephone: (303) 927–3311.

Order: Cistercian (Trappist) monks (Roman Catholic).

Accommodations: Ten guests in the guest house in single and twin rooms, all with shared bath.

Meals: Guests prepare their own meals in the guest house kitchenette.

Charges: No set fee; freewill offerings accepted.

Directions: If driving from Denver, take I–70 to Glenwood Springs, then Highway 82 from Glenwood Springs to Old Snowmass, which is two and a half miles past Basalt. Turn right at the intersection where there is a Conoco gas station. Then go straight for about seven and a half miles, bearing right at the one crossroad. At the end of seven and a half miles you will see a sign for the monastery on the left side of the road. Turn left at the sign onto the monastery road and travel one mile to the gatehouse, which is next to a large wooden arch spanning the road.

If using public transportation, there is air service to Aspen. Amtrak train service goes to Glenwood Springs, and Trailways buses go to Glenwood Springs, Basalt, and Aspen. Arrange with the guest master in advance to be met at the airport or depot.

Description: Set in a valley at an elevation of 8,000 feet, St. Benedict's Abbey property is extensive and includes a ranch, streams, hills, aspen forests, and meadowlands. The abbey abuts a national forest, and the nearest neighbors (none closer than a mile) are ranchers. The monks work on their own ranch and in their greenhouse and egg farm.

Points of Interest: The abbey is close to Aspen, an old silver-mining town that is now a ski center as well as a cultural center.

Special Note: The guest house is usually booked several months in advance. Groups are welcome to use the "ranch house" for winter or spring retreats. A descriptive brochure is available from the abbey's guest master.

CONVENT OF ST. BIRGITTA

Vikingsborg
Runkenhage Road
Tokeneke Trail
Darien, Connecticut 06820

Telephone: (203) 655–1068.

Order: Sisters of St. Birgitta (Roman Catholic).

Accommodations: Nine guests in the guest house in single and twin rooms, some with private baths.

Meals: Three meals daily.

Charges: From $25 to $32 per person per day for room and meals; from $50 to $64 per person per weekend.

Directions: By car from New York, New Jersey, and southern Connecticut, take the Connecticut Turnpike to Exit 12; turn right onto Tokeneke Road. Proceed a half mile on Tokeneke Road to intersection island; bear right around island to Old Farm Road and follow a half mile to Tokeneke Trail. Bear right on Tokeneke Trail and proceed a half mile to Runkenhage Road (note green shield-shaped sign on the left of road). Turn onto Runken-hage Road to first driveway on the right (about fifty feet from turn); drive through two sets of stone posts in direction of sign reading "Vikingsborg."

By public transportation, take the New Haven Railroad to Darien, Connecticut. Taxis are available at the station at each train arrival. The convent is about one and three-quarter miles from the station.

History: The patron and namesake of this order is St. Birgitta of Sweden, a Swedish noblewoman born in 1302 and widely known in medieval times through the reading of her *Revelations.* The order flourished in northern Europe during the Middle Ages but nearly became extinct following the Reformation. The sisters began an era of resurgence and growth at the turn of the century, and in 1957 four sisters arrived in Darien to take up residence at Vikingsborg.

Description: The spacious guest house is close to woodland walks and gardens, and guests enjoy "the peace, silence, serenity, and beauty which surrounds the whole place . . . ."

Points of Interest: Vikingsborg is on the Long Island Sound.

Special Note: The convent does not schedule retreats, but retreat groups of all denominations are welcome to come with their own director for days of recollection, meditation, study, discussion, or workshop. Literature and information is available from the convent's guest sister.

ST. ANSELM'S ABBEY
4501 South Dakota Avenue, N.E.
Washington, D.C. 20017

Telephone: (202) 269-2300.

Order: Benedictine monks (Roman Catholic).

Accommodations: Eight men in the monastery in single rooms, all with shared bath.

Meals: Three meals daily.

Charges: An offering of $25 per day for room and meals is suggested.

Directions: By public transportation, take the Metro to Brookland-CUA (red line), then any R bus to 14th Street and Michigan Avenue.

History: In 1923 five Americans, intent on living as Benedictine monks in Washington, went to the Scottish

Abbey of Fort Augustus. The following year, after completing their novitiate training, they returned to Washington with several monks from Fort Augustus and established St. Anselm's in a wooden farmhouse on a tract of land not far from the Catholic University of America. In 1930 the monks moved into a newly built English Tudor-style monastery. A newer, more modern wing was added in 1964. A day school for boys was opened in 1942.

Description: The red brick abbey church with its wooden choir stalls and stained-glass windows is the nucleus of the abbey property. The abbey's grounds are a peaceful refuge in urban Washington.

Points of Interest: The new and efficient Washington Metro provides fast and easy access to the city's many monuments and museums.

CONVENT OF ST. HELENA
3042 Eagle Drive
Augusta, Georgia 30916–5645

Telephone: (404) 798–5201.

Order: Order of St. Helena (Episcopal).

Accommodations: Twenty-three guests in single rooms in three guest houses; most rooms have shared bath.

Meals: Three meals daily.

Charges: Freewill offerings accepted.

Directions: Driving directions given on request.
   If using public transportation, there is plane and bus service to Augusta. Arrange in advance to be met on arrival.

History: The sisters arrived in Augusta in 1961, first taking up residence in a small log house that had been lent to them. In 1966, a gift of ten acres was given to the order, and a chapel, convent, and guest house were constructed on the site.

Description: Located on a partially wooded hill just south of Augusta, the convent has views of the city's skyline and of South Carolina across the Savannah River. A contemporary design and use of concrete, wood, and glass have given the convent a feeling of simplicity and spaciousness.

Special Note: Open conducted retreats are occasionally given at the convent, and information on these may be gotten from the guest sister.

MONASTERY OF THE VISITATION
Maryfield
2055 Ridgedale Drive
Snellville, Georgia 30278

Telephone: (404) 972–1060.

Order: Visitation nuns (Roman Catholic).

Accommodations: Three women in the monastery, each with a single room and all with shared bath.

Meals: Three meals daily.

Charges: $15 per person per day for room and meals.

Directions: If driving from Atlanta, take I–285 east to Route 78 (Exit 30—Athens) to Route 124.
   If flying, the closest airport is Hartford International Airport.

History: The Order of the Visitation was founded in France in 1610 by St: Francis de Sales and St. Frances de Chantel. This is an order of cloistered, contemplative nuns.

Description: Maryfield has twenty-six acres of natural beauty that include two wooded areas and a pond. Guests have access to these as well as a small library and reading room.

Special Note: The retreat area within the monastery enclosure is open to women retreatants for a period of two to eight days. For a brochure and more information, contact the monastery's guest sister.

BETHLEHEM HOUSE

Convent of St. Anne
1125 N. La Salle Drive
Chicago, Illinois 60610

Telephone: (312) 944–9641 or 642–3638.

Order: Sisters of St. Anne (Episcopal).

Accommodations: Five guests in single rooms, one of which has a private bath.

Meals: No meals for individual guests on private retreats. (Guests participating in weekend, group retreats are given meals Friday evening through Sunday midday.)

Charges: $20 to $25 per night for single room for an individual guest. ($75 for room—two nights—and six meals for those participating in a weekend retreat.)

Directions: Contact the guest sister if driving directions are needed.

If using public transportation, the nearest subway stop is at Clark and Division.

History: The Order of St. Anne was begun by a Cowley Father, the Reverend Frederick Powell, in 1910 in Massachusetts. Since its founding, the order has grown to include houses in a number of states, and the sisters have undertaken a variety of charitable works.

Description: Bethlehem House is a small island of tranquility in the midst of downtown Chicago. The house is in the virtual shadow of the Church of the Ascension. This church has been at the forefront of the Anglo-Catholic movement in the Episcopal Church since 1869.

Points of Interest: All of downtown Chicago, its museums, historic sites, and restaurants are at the doorstep of Bethlehem House.

Special Note: The guest sister can provide information on group/weekend retreats.

ST. MEINRAD ARCHABBEY GUEST HOUSE
St. Meinrad, Indiana 47577

Telephone: (812) 357–6585.

Order: Benedictine monks (Roman Catholic).

Accommodations: Fifty-two guests in twenty-six twin-bedded rooms, each with private bath.

Meals: Three meals daily.

Charges: Rooms are $18 per day, single occupancy, and $21 per day, double occupancy. Meals are approximately $7 per day.

Directions: Located on I–64, the abbey is sixty miles from Louisville, Kentucky, and fifty miles from Evansville, Indiana.
   If using public transportation, there is plane service to Louisville and to Evansville. Contact the guest master for more details.

History: St. Meinrad Archabbey was founded in 1854 by monks of Einsiedeln Abbey, Switzerland. Originally the monks ministered among the German Catholic population, later expanding their efforts to work among the Indians and education. A college and seminary are at the abbey today.

Description: The abbey is picturesquely perched above the banks of the nearby river. Guests are welcome to join the monks in worship in the abbey church, which is large, historic, and newly renovated.

Special Note: Contact the guest master for information about group retreats.

MISSISSIPPI ABBEY
8400 Abbey Hill
Dubuque, Iowa 52001

Telephone: (319) 582–2595 (call between 9:00 and 11:30 A.M.).

Order: Cistercian (Trappestine) nuns (Roman Catholic).

Accommodations: Eleven women in single and twin rooms in three houses, all with shared bath.

Meals: The nuns provide food for all the retreat houses, and guests cook their own meals.

Charges: Freewill offering accepted.

Directions: If driving from Dubuque, take Locust Street (Route 151/61 south) to Highway 52. Turn left (south) onto Highway 52 and travel for about five or six miles. The abbey sign will be on the right, directing a *left* turn onto a gravel road. It is about a twenty-minute drive from Dubuque.

If using public transportation, there is plane and bus service to Dubuque.

History: The history of the Cistercian nuns closely parallels that of the monks of the same order. The Cistercians are an eleventh-century reform of the Benedictine order. A further reform was initiated at the abbey of La Trappe, France, in 1664. Trappestine nuns (as they are often called) from Ireland and England opened an American foundation in Wrentham, Massachusetts, and in 1968 twelve nuns from Wrentham opened Mississippi Abbey.

Description: Mississippi Abbey has about 580 acres of property full of bluffs, woods, and creeks that guests are free to explore. The nuns run a farm on which they produce their own food, and their main industry is the manufacture and sale of Trappestine Creamy Caramels.

Points of Interest: Marquette explored this area, and Dubuque was the first Roman Catholic archdiocese west of the Mississippi River. The Stone House (one of the guest houses) is an old country farmhouse dating from the mid-nineteenth century.

Special Note: The Stone House is open from March to November 1st. The retreat house and cabin are open year-round. Retreats are usually booked two months in advance, although there are sometimes last-minute cancellations. Reservations are not accepted during the months of November and December due to the busy schedule at the candy house at that time.

BETHLEHEM PRIORY
430 N. Limestone Street
Lexington, Kentucky 40508–1874

Telephone: (606) 252–4354.

Order: Benedictine monks/Servants of Jesus (Episcopal).

Accommodations: Five men in the monastery in single and twin rooms, all with shared bath.

Meals: Three meals daily.

Charges: "As the spirit moves."

Directions: If driving from Main Street, go north on Limestone Street, past 4th Street. The priory is about eight houses on the right.
   If using public transportation, take the North Limestone bus.

History: The Servants of Jesus was instituted in 1981. Its members lead a life of prayer, study, and service to others. The monks work among the city's poor providing food, educational tutoring, and other assistance.

Description: Located in Lexington's historic district, the priory is housed in Henry Clay's office building, which dates from the 1840s.

Points of Interest: The University of Kentucky, Mary Todd Lincoln's house, and the historic opera house are all near the priory.

Special Note: Guests are asked to call in advance to see if room is available, as a large number of oblates and associates visit regularly.

GETHSEMANI ABBEY
Trappist, Kentucky 40051

Telephone: (502) 549–3117.

Order: Cistercian (Trappist) monks (Roman Catholic).

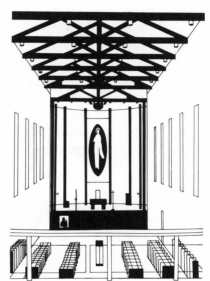

Accommodations: Eighteen men in single rooms and shared baths in the guest house.

Meals: Three meals daily.

Charges: Freewill donations accepted.

Directions: If driving, take Route 31E south from Bardtown, Kentucky, then turn left on Route 247.

If using public transportation, contact the guest master for information about van service from Louisville or Lexington.

History: The Cistercians are a reform of the Benedictine order dating to the eleventh century. In the seventeenth century, a further reform was led by the French Abbot de Rance of La Grande Trappe Abbey. These Cistercians of the Strict Observance have since been popularly known as "Trappists." A group of Trappist monks journeyed from France and settled in Kentucky in 1848.

Description: The abbey has an extensive property on

which the monks farm and tend to other work such as the production of cheese and fruit cake. Guests are welcome to walk in the gardens or the woodlands and to join the monks for worship in the large and historic abbey church.

Points of Interest: Gethsemani Abbey was the home of Thomas Merton.

Special Note: The weekend retreat is from Friday afternoon to Sunday afternoon (or Monday morning). The midweek retreat is from Monday afternoon to Friday morning. Brochures and further information are available from the abbey's guest master.

ALL SAINTS CONVENT

P.O. Box 3106
Catonsville, Maryland 21228

Telephone: (301) 747–6767.

Order: All Saints Sisters
of the Poor (Episcopal).

Accommodations: Nine
women in the convent
in single rooms, all with
shared bath.

Meals: Three meals
daily.

Charges: Freewill offering (but $70 per person
per weekend will cover
the convent's costs).

Directions: If driving,
take I–95 and exit at
Catonsville exit to Roll-
ing Road. When Rolling Road meets Hilton Avenue,
make a very sharp left. The convent is at the end of Hilton
Avenue.

If using public transportation, take plane to Baltimore-
Washington International Airport or train to BWI Airport
Rail Station. Arrange ahead for possible pickup on arrival.

History: Founded in London in 1851, the sisters were
named for the parish they served: All Saints, Margaret
Street. In 1872 a group was sent to Baltimore to work
among the city's poor, and in 1917 a gift was made of

the Catonsville property. For more than a century the sisters have carried on a number of charitable works including schools, a summer day camp for inner-city children, a home for elderly women, care for the terminally ill, and retreat work. The All Saints Scriptorium is widely known, and greeting cards are sold at the Convent Card Shop and by mail order.

Description: The beautiful stone Gothic Revival chapel and convent are set on eighty-eight acres of natural woodlands, all of which is surrounded by state park lands.

Points of Interest: The convent abuts Patapsco State Park where there are numerous trails for walks and hikes.

Special Note: St. Gabriel's Retreat House on the convent grounds offers retreats for groups of up to twenty-five persons. Contact the guest sister for brochures and further information on individual retreats in the convent and group retreats at St. Gabriel's.

ANNUNCIATION MONASTERY
P.O. Box 21238
Catonsville, Maryland 21228

Telephone: (301) 747–6140 (call between 9:30 A.M. and 7:00 P.M.).

Order: All Saints Sisters of the Poor (Episcopal).

Accommodations: Four men in the monastery, each with single room and all with shared bath.

Meals: Three meals daily.

Charges: Freewill offering (but $70 per weekend will cover the costs to lodge a guest).

Directions: If driving, take I–95 and exit at Catonsville exit to Rolling Road. When Rolling Road meets Hilton Avenue, make a very sharp left. All Saints Convent and the monastery are at the end of Hilton Avenue.

If using public transportation, take plane to Baltimore-Washington International Airport or train to BWI Airport Rail Station. Arrangement can be made for pickup on arrival.

Description: Annunciation Monastery is a ministry of the All Saints Sisters of the Poor. It is a wood-frame house on the property of the sisters' motherhouse. The monastery is surrounded by nearly ninety wooded and landscaped acres, and, beyond that, state park lands.

Points of Interest: Patapsco State Park, contiguous with the All Saints property, offers opportunities for walks and hikes.

Special Note: The resident chaplain may be contacted for a brochure, map, and more information.

EMERY HOUSE
Emery Lane
West Newbury, Massachusetts 01985

Telephone: (508) 462–7940.

Order: Cowley Fathers (Episcopal).

Accommodations: At least twelve guests in the guest house and in hermitages, some with private baths.

Meals: Three meals daily.

Charges: $30 per person per day for room and meals.

Directions: If driving, take I–95 to Route 113; continue west for one and a quarter miles to Emery Lane on your right.
   If using public transportation, there is Greyhound bus service to Newburyport.

History: This farmhouse, which dates back to the eighteenth century, was given to the Society of St. John the Evangelist (Cowley Fathers) in 1948. In recent years the house has been used as a retreat, and in 1987 the

Chapel of the Transfiguration and a cluster of hermitages were added.

Description: Emery House is situated on over one hundred acres of field and woodland bordered by the Merrimack and Artichoke rivers.

Points of Interest: About a half mile down the road from the house is a four-hundred-acre state park with trail. The historic seaport city of Newburyport is at the mouth of the Merrimack River. Newburyport has become a model for historic preservation projects.

Special Note: Group retreats are given at Emery House on occasion; a calendar may be gotten from the guest master. Reservations must be made in writing, and a nonrefundable deposit of $30 is necessary to secure a reservation.

GLASTONBURY ABBEY
16 Hull Street
Hingham, Massachusetts 02043

Telephone: (617)
749–2155 (best to
call Monday to Fri-
day, 8 A.M. to 2
P.M.).

Order: Benedic-
tine monks (Roman
Catholic).

Accommodations:
Thirty guests in two
guest houses. There
are twenty-three
rooms (single and
twin), some of which
have private baths.

Meals: Three meals daily.

Charges: Suggested minimum offering of $25 to $30 per
night for room and meals.

Directions: By car from Boston, take I–93 south (Southeast Expressway) to Route 3 south (to Cape Cod) to Exit
14, "Route 228, Rockland-Hingham." Follow Route 228
north (Main Street, Hingham) about seven miles to the
abbey. Driving I–95 from Rhode Island, Connecticut, and
New York, take I–93 north (toward Boston). Follow I–93
north to Route 3 south (to Cape Cod), getting off Route
3 at Exit 14, "Route 228, Rockland-Hingham." Take
Route 228 north (Main Street, Hingham) for about seven

miles to the abbey. If driving from the Massachusetts Turnpike (I–90), get off the pike at I–95 and go south. This road turns into I–93 north—be sure to *stay on this road.* Follow I–93 to Route 3 south (to Cape Cod), getting off Route 3 at Exit 14 (as above).

By public transportation from Boston, take the "T" (subway) Red Line Braintree train to Quincy Center Station. Then take the "220 Hingham" bus to the last stop (Station Street). Call the abbey for pick up if prior arrangement had been made. An alternate means of public transportation from Boston is the Plymouth & Brockton Busline, which leaves from the Greyhound Bus Terminal (Park Square) in Boston or at South Station. Take a "Scituate" bus. Buy a "Hingham–Main Street" ticket. Ask to be let off at the monastery (last stop in Hingham). This is a very limited bus service, with no runs whatsoever on the weekend.

History: At the invitation of the late Cardinal Cushing, monks from Benet Lake, Wisconsin, founded this monastery in 1954. It was the first Benedictine monastery in the Commonwealth of Massachusetts.

Description: The abbey is located on sixty wooded acres less than two miles from the Atlantic Ocean. The guest houses, Stonecrest and Whitting House, are informal and comfortable homes, noninstitutional in character.

Points of Interest: Hingham is a historic town (founded in 1635) just sixteen miles south of Boston. The Old Ship Church (1681) in Hingham is the last remaining Puritan meetinghouse in America.

Special Note: In addition to extending hospitality to individual guests, the abbey has a full schedule of group retreats. A calendar and further information is available from the abbey's guest master.

MONASTERY OF ST. MARY AND ST. JOHN
980 Memorial Drive
Cambridge, Massachusetts 02138

Telephone: (617) 547–7330 or 876–3037.

Order: Cowley Fathers (Episcopal).

Accommodations: Sixteen guests in single rooms in the guest house. Each room has its own sink; toilets and showers are nearby.

Meals: Three meals daily.

Charges: Suggested donation of $30 per person per day for room and meals (see special note below).

Directions: If driving from Route 128, take Route 2 east. Make a left onto Memorial Drive. The monastery will be on the left.

If using public transportation, take the "T" (subway) Red Line to Harvard Square. Walk down J.F. Kennedy Street to Memorial Drive. Make a right onto Memorial Drive.

History: The Society of St. John the Evangelist, the oldest monastic community in the Anglican communion, was founded by the Reverend Richard Meux Benson in 1866.

The society was begun near Oxford, England, in the village of Cowley—St. John. For that reason, members of the society have been popularly called the "Cowley Fathers." In 1870 the fathers came to Boston, Massachusetts, later settling their American motherhouse across the Charles River in Cambridge.

Description: The monastery was designed by the architect Ralph Adams Cram, and the granite church is considered by many to be one of his masterpieces. The guest house, church, and monastery are all attached and occupy a small plot of land. Guests are free to walk along the Charles River across the road and to enjoy the wider expanse and fresh air.

Points of Interest: The monastery is virtually on the doorstep of Harvard University, and the "T" (subway) in Harvard Square provides easy access to the sights of Boston and its environs.

Special Note: The guest house is closed on Mondays until 6:00 P.M. and during the months of July and August. Reservations must be made in writing, and a nonrefundable deposit of $30 is necessary to secure a reservation. If it is not possible for the guest to give the suggested donation, arrangements can be made with the guest master. Group retreats are given at the monastery, and a brochure, calendar, and other information are available from the guest master.

ST. BENEDICT PRIORY
250 Still River Road
Still River, Massachusetts 01467

Telephone: (508) 456-3221.

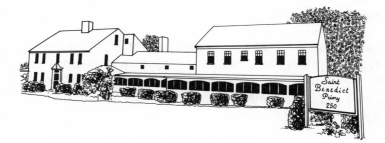

Order: Benedictine monks (Roman Catholic).

Accommodations: Sixty guests (in the guest house) in single and twin-bedded rooms, some with private baths.

Meals: Three meals daily.

Charges: $25 per person per day for room and meals.

Directions: If driving, take I–495 to Route 117 west to Route 110 north (Still River Road).
   If using public transportation, take Trailways bus or commuter rail from Boston to Ayer, Massachusetts.

History: This community was formed in 1940 and moved to Still River in 1958. The monastery has recently been joined to the Swiss-American Congregation of Benedictines. The monks publish books and offer hospitality to guests and visitors.

Description: The priory is situated on eighty-five acres of woodland and farmland overlooking the scenic Nashoba Valley. The monastery is a 300-year-old Colonial home that has been decorated and furnished with paintings and chairs of the period. The guest house is about 250 years old. Guests are welcome to join the monks at worship, where the traditional Gregorian plainchant is sung.

Points of Interest: Historic Lexington and Concord are near the priory, as is Fruitlands Museum. Fruitlands is the remains of an eighteenth-century Utopian Transcendental community, which, as the priory, overlooks the valley.

ST. JOSEPH'S ABBEY RETREAT HOUSE
Spencer, Massachusetts 01562

Telephone: (508) 885–3010.

Order: Cistercian (Trappist) monks (Roman Catholic).

Accommodations: Eleven men in the retreat house, each in single room with private bath.

Meals: Three meals daily.

Charges: Free offerings, but the average minimum has been about $25 to $30 per day for room and meals.

Directions: If driving, take the Massachusetts Turnpike (I–90) to Exit 10 (Auburn). Then go onto Route 12 and Route 20 west for three miles. Go right onto Route 56 to Leicester (eight miles), then left on Route 9 to Spencer (nine miles). From Route 9 make a right onto Route 31 to the abbey (five miles).

If flying, take a flight to Worcester Airport and then a taxi to the abbey.

History: This community is the descendant of the Abbey of Our Lady of the Valley, Cumberland, Rhode Island. After the Rhode Island abbey burned in 1950, the monks resettled in Spencer. The new abbey, with its exterior of fieldstones hauled from the surrounding farmlands, was built by the monks in 1952–53 under the supervision of an architect and contractor. Today the monks support themselves in part through the production and sale of Trappist Preserves. The Holy Rood Guild at the abbey designs and sells liturgical vestments.

Description: The abbey property includes nearly two thousand acres of woodland and cultivated fields. The retreat house is attached to the monastery and abbey church, where guests are encouraged to join the monks at services.

Special Note: A weekend retreat begins on Friday afternoon and ends on Sunday after lunch. The midweek retreat extends from Monday afternoon until Friday morning. One conference is given each day. Reservations must be made in advance. Literature and more information may be gotten from the abbey's guest master.

ST. SCHOLASTICA PRIORY
North Main Street
P.O. Box 606
Petersham, Massachusetts 01366

Telephone: (508) 724–3213 and 724–3217.

Order: Benedictine nuns (Roman Catholic).

Accommodations: Five guests or more in single rooms, all with shared bath.

Meals: Three meals daily.

Charges: Freewill offerings accepted.

Directions: By car from Boston, take Route 2 west to Athol/Petersham exit (Route 32). Make a right turn at the bottom of the ramp onto Route 32 south. Monastery is on the right side of the road after the Harvard University Forest and before the Petersham Country Club.

If using public transportation, there is bus service from Boston to Orange or Gardiner, Massachusetts. One of the nuns can meet you if prior arrangement has been made.

History: The newly founded St. Scholastica Priory is unique in that it has a close association with the Benedictine monks of St. Mary's Priory in the United Kingdom. Like the monks at St. Mary's, the nuns use a mixture of Latin Gregorian chant and some English in their liturgy. This is a contemplative monastery that supports itself by the operation of the Priory Bakery, St. Bede's Publications, and contributions.

Description: The monastery is housed in a Scottish manor house built in 1929. A new monastery with larger guest quarters is being planned. Petersham is in Massachusetts' scenic Pioneer Valley.

Points of Interest: The priory is close to the immense (128 square miles) Quabbin Reservoir, where visitors may enjoy scenic drives and panoramas as well as opportunities for hiking and fishing.

ST. AUGUSTINE'S HOUSE
3316 East Drahner Road
Oxford, Michigan 48051

Telephone: (313) 628–5155.

Order: Servants of Christ (Lutheran).

Accommodations: Five men in single rooms in the monastery, all with shared bath.

Meals: Three meals daily.

Charges: Suggested donation of $15 to $20 per person per day for room and meals.

Directions: By car from Detroit and Pontiac, take I–75 north to M24. Continue north on M24 and take a right on East Drahner Road. St. Augustine's House will be on the left after two and a half miles. From Flint and Lapeer, take M24 south and make a left onto East Drahner Road.

If using public transportation, take a plane to Detroit and then limousine service to Pontiac. There is also bus service to Pontiac and train service to Lapeer.

History: This, the only Lutheran monastery in the United States, was founded in 1958 by the Reverend Arthur Carl Kreinheder. Following World War II there was a rekindled interest in monastic life among Lutherans, especially in Europe. This community, which is affiliated with a Swedish order, is an outgrowth of that movement.

Description: The monks own a number of pleasant acres in a rural setting. The retreat house, which stands on a hillside, has views for many miles. Both it and the monastery are near the Chapel of the Visitation.

Special Note: Guest information and maps are available from the guest master.

ST. GREGORY'S ABBEY
56500 Abbey Road
Three Rivers, Michigan 49093

Telephone: (616) 244–5893 (9:30–11:15 A.M. and 2:15–4:30 P.M. Eastern Standard Time).

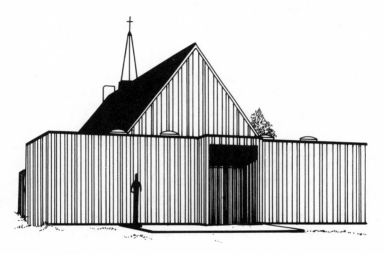

Order: Benedictine monks (Episcopal).

Accommodations: Ten men in single rooms in a wing of the monastery. There are also accommodations for six women in single rooms in St. Denys Guest House. There are shared baths in each facility.

Meals: Three meals daily for men staying in the monastery. Women's meals are self-prepared in the guest house.

Charges: Freewill offerings accepted.

Directions: If driving, take I–94 to Kalamazoo, then U.S. 131 south. At Three Rivers, go right on Route 105, then right on Abbey Road (Route 103).

If using public transportation, take a plane, train, or bus to Kalamazoo, where a monk can meet you for transportation to the abbey.

History: The Anglican Benedictine monks of Nashdom Abbey, England, founded an American branch in Indiana in 1939. The monks moved to Three Rivers in 1946, and in 1969 St. Gregory's Priory was raised to the status of a fully independent abbey.

Description: The abbey, its church, monastery, guest house, and other buildings are in a parklike setting surrounded by woods and farmland.

Special Note: Reservations should be made as far in advance as is practical. The normal length of stay is from two days to one week. Weekend retreats for groups are scheduled from September through May. The abbey may be building an additional guest house. For an update, brochures, and further information, contact the guest master.

CHRISTINA HOUSE HERMITAGES

P.O. Box 619
Abbey Lane
Pevely, Missouri 63070

Telephone: (314) 479–3697.

Order: Benedictine monks (Roman Catholic).

Accommodations: Five guests in five hermitages, each with a private bath. (Two more guests may be accommodated in two of the hermitages furnished with trundle beds.)

Meals: No meals are provided. Each hermitage is equipped with appliances and utensils for light cooking.

Charges: $12.50 per person for each twenty-four-hour period.

Directions: By car from St. Louis, take I–55 south to the Pevely exit. Turn east, cross Highway 61–67, and continue one mile.

Using public transportation, take a bus from St. Louis to Crystal City, Missouri.

History: Christina means "little Christ," and in dedication to Christ this house was opened in 1977. Through the efforts and inspiration of Sr. Miriam Clare Stoll, S.P., this project has flourished and grown to include five hermitages.

Description: The hermitages are underground, each being built forty feet from the other to assure greater solitude. All overlook the Mississippi River and the setting is one of peace and scenic beauty.

Points of Interest: The house and St. Pius X Abbey are just thirty miles from St. Louis, its arch and cultural attractions.

ST. LOUIS PRIORY

500 South Mason Road
St. Louis, Missouri 63141

Telephone: (314) 434–2557.

Order: Benedictine monks (Roman Catholic).

Accommodations: Four men in the monastery, each in a single room. Two rooms have private baths and the other two have a shared bath.

Meals: Three meals daily.

Charges: $10 per person per day for room and meals.

Directions: The priory is located two blocks north of U.S. 40 (I–64), west of I–270 on Mason Road.
   If using public transportation, guests arriving in St. Louis by air, Amtrak, or Greyhound will be met if prior arrangement has been made for pickup on arrival.

History: This priory of the English Benedictine Congregation was begun in 1955 by monks of Ampleforth Abbey, England. From the start, the monks have had a school for boys here.

Description: The monks are fortunate to have a number of acres of lawn and woods just west of the city. The focal point of the property is the strikingly modern priory church.

Points of Interest: The Gateway Arch, the Old Cathedral, St. Louis Cathedral, and the other sights of St. Louis are within easy access of the priory.

CHRIST THE KING PRIORY
P.O. Box 528
Schuyler, Nebraska 68661

Telephone: (402) 352–2177.

Order: Benedictine monks (Roman Catholic).

Accommodations: Seven men in the monastery in four rooms (one single and three twin). Each room has a private bath.

Meals: Three meals daily.

Charges: At least $10 per day for room and meals.

Directions: By car, take Highway 30. At its intersection with Highway 15, turn north and continue four miles.

Using public transportation, there is plane service to Omaha (sixty-five miles west). Greyhound and Red Arrow provide bus service to Schuyler.

History: The Benedictine Missionary Congregation of St. Ottilien was founded in Germany in the late nineteenth century. In 1935 the Benedictine Mission House was opened in Schuyler. The congregation has missions worldwide, and the priory is its development and education office in the United States.

Description: Completed in 1979, the monastery is unique in that it is literally set into the natural landscape of the area, its roof and outer walls covered by a verdant carpet of grass. The priory is surrounded by a broad expanse of Nebraska farmland.

Points of Interest: Omaha is the home of the Strategic Aerospace Museum, the Western Heritage Museum, and the Joslyn Art Musuem. Fr. Flanagan's Boys Town is just west of Omaha.

THE COMMON
Old Street Road
Peterborough, New Hampshire 03458

Telephone: (603) 924–6060.

Order: Discalced Carmelite friars (Roman Catholic).

Accommodations: Thirty guests in the guest house in eighteen rooms (single, twin, and triple). Nearly all the rooms have shared bath.

Meals: Three meals daily.

Charges: $30 per person per weekday for room and meals; $75 per person for a weekend (Friday to Sunday).

Directions: If driving, take Route 101 to junction with Route 123 on the east side of Peterborough at the yellow blinking light. Do *not* follow Route 123. Instead, drive north on Old Street Road for one mile. An oval sign for ''The Common'' will be on your left. If you reach Peterborough on Route 202, turn east on Route 101 and follow the preceding directions.

If using public transportation, there is air service (Eastern Express) and bus service (Greyhound's Vermont Transit) to Keene. Arrange in advance with guest master for pickup on arrival.

History: This is the site of the original town common (1752); later was used for farmland, and in 1898 was made a summer estate. In time, this became a preparatory school for girls, then a seminary, and, in the late 1960s, a retreat center. The Heritage Room at the Common illustrates and documents the fascinating history of this place.

Description: The Common has 175 acres of woodlands and meadows. There are sweeping views of Mount Monadnock to the west and Pack Monadnock Mountain to the east.

Points of Interest: Mount Monadnock is the second most climbed mountain in the world. Pack Monadnock has an auto road to the summit, where there are fine views of the region. A path of granite steps leads from the Common to All Saints Episcopal Church at the foot of East Hill. Often said to be the most beautiful church of its size in America, Ralph Adams Cram was the architect; Transitional Gothic, the style; and local granite, the building material.

Peterborough is the inspiration for Thornton Wilder's *Our Town.* The town's Unitarian Church is said to be designed by Charles Bulfinch. The Cathedral of the Pines is in the neighboring town of Rindge.

Special Note: In addition to receiving individual guests, the Common offers a number of group retreats annually. Information and a calendar may be obtained from the Common's guest master.

ST. PAUL'S ABBEY
Queen of Peace Retreat House
Newton, New Jersey 07860

Telephone: (201) 383–2470 or 383–0660.

Order: Benedictine monks (Roman Catholic).

Accommodations: Eighty guests in single rooms in the monastery and in the guest house, all with shared bath.

Meals: Three meals daily.

Charges: Please consult the guest master for charges.

Directions: By car from the east or west, take I–80 to Exit 25, Route 206 north, Newton. Go north on Route 206 to the 107 mile post. The abbey is about a half mile from the marker. From the south, take I–287 or Route 202 to Route 206 north and follow Route 206 as above. From the north, take I–84 to Milford, Pennsylvania, and follow Route 206 south. The abbey is one mile south of the town of Newton.

By bus, take the Lakeland Bus Lines (platform 407, upper level of Manhattan's Port Authority bus terminal).

71

Ask the driver to let you off at St. Paul's Abbey. The retreat house is across the road from the abbey gift shop.

History: This house of the missionary Congregation of St. Ottilien was begun in 1925 under the auspices of the German Archabbey of St. Ottilien. The monks are engaged in missionary work in Africa and support themselves at the abbey by growing and selling Christmas trees.

Description: Queen of Peace Retreat House at the abbey provides Benedictine hospitality to many visitors each year. Guests are free to walk about and to enjoy the five hundred acres of woodland on the abbey property.

Points of Interest: The abbey is about fifty miles from New York City and just a few miles from Waterloo Village and the scenic Delaware Water Gap National Recreation Area.

Special Note: In addition to welcoming individual guests, the abbey offers a full schedule of group retreats. Brochures and further information are available from the abbey's guest master.

ST. MICHAEL'S FOREST VALLEY PRIORY
P.O. Box 43
Tajique, New Mexico 87057

Telephone: (505) 384–2435.

Order: Order of Agape and
Reconciliation (Episcopal/
ecumenical).

Accommodations: Twelve
guests (in the priory and in
the guest house) in single
rooms, some with private
baths.

Meals: Meals may be provided for guests, or guests
may bring their own gro-
ceries and use one of the
kitchens.

Charges: $20 per person per day.

Directions: If driving from Albuquerque, take I–40 east
to Tijeras. When you see the large cement plant on your
right, take the Tijeras off-ramp to Route 14 south (turn
right). Where Route 14 south "dead ends," turn right
(west) toward the mountains. In Tajique, turn right (west)
at San Antonio de Padua Church, 4th of July Canyon
Road. Priory is five miles west on the right side.

If using public transportation, the nearest airport is
Albuquerque International Airport. If traveling by bus,
Greyhound has service to Estancia, fourteen miles from
the priory. Advance arrangements can be made for pickup
at terminals on arrival ($15 transportation donation).

History: This semimonastic order was founded under the auspices of the Episcopal Church in 1972. Both contemplative and active, the order's membership includes Episcopalians, Roman Catholics, Orthodox, and Protestants and includes men and women clergy and laypersons, both married and celibate.

Description: The priory, located on sixty wooded acres in the Manzano Mountains (elevation 7,200 feet) is fifty miles southeast of Albuquerque. Those staying at the priory have the privileged use of fifty contiguous acres of forested land.

Points of Interest: New Mexico is a tricultural state (Indian, Spanish, and Anglo). Visitors will find a number of historical sites within a twenty-five-mile radius of St. Michael's.

Special Note: Silent, nondirected retreats are offered to groups visiting the priory. Guests are advised to send in an early application and a $50 nonrefundable deposit (which will be applied to the suggested donation). Descriptive brochures are available on request.

ABBEY OF THE GENESEE

River Road
Piffard, New York 14533

Telephone: (716) 243–0660.

Order: Cistercian (Trappist) monks (Roman Catholic).

Accommodations: Sixteen men in single rooms in Bethlehem House, all with shared bath. In addition, there are accommodations for up to thirty-two guests (men and women) in Bethany House and Cana House, all with shared bath.

Meals: Three meals daily in Bethlehem House. Guests may use the kitchen in Bethany and Cana houses to prepare their own meals.

Charges: No fixed fee; freewill donations accepted.

Directions: The Genesee Expressway, Route 390, provides easy access by car to Genesco, New York. Traveling north or south along Route 390, take Exit 8 for Genesco.

At the Genesco exit, proceed west on Route 20A. Turn right at Highway 63, north. In Piffard, turn right at River Road, north. A sign for the abbey will indicate the turn onto River Road. If traveling west on the New York State Thruway, exit at interchange 46, proceeding south on Route 390 to Exit 8, as previously outlined.

If using public transportation, the nearest airport is Monroe County Airport in Rochester. There is also Amtrak service to Rochester as well as Greyhound and Trailways bus service. There is Trailways bus service from Rochester to Genesco. From there, taxi service, though expensive, is available. If necessary, the abbey can provide transportation from Genesco if a previous arrangement is made.

History: Trappist monks from Gethsemane Abbey in Kentucky arrived in the Genesee Valley in 1951, having accepted the gift of a tract of land. The community originally lived in what is now Bethlehem Retreat House. The abbey church, built of stone and designed to express ''an appropriate blend of modern and traditional elements,'' was completed in 1975.

Description: Across the road from Bethlehem House is Bethany, a stately nineteenth-century cobblestone house. Cana is a modern wood-frame family dwelling just down the road. Each guest house is about a mile from the abbey church.

Points of Interest: Letchworth State Park is just south of the abbey.

Special Note: Brochures and guidelines on all three guest houses are available from the abbey's guest master.

CONVENT OF ST. HELENA
P.O. Box 426
Vails Gate, New York 12584

Telephone: (914) 562–0592.

Order: Order of St. Helena (Episcopal).

Accommodations: Twenty-four guests in the guest house in eight single and eight twin rooms, all with shared bath.

Meals: Three meals daily.

Charges: Suggested donation of at least $25 per person per day for room and meals.

Directions: From points south, take the New York State Thruway north to Exit 16 at Harriman. Take Route 32 north through Central Valley and several more small towns to Vails Gate, where there is a five-way intersection with a traffic light and a Hess gas station ahead and to the left. Turn right onto Route 94 (east). After the next traffic light (Forge Hill Road), the convent is the first drive on the right. If traveling from I-84, take Exit 7S, marked

Route 300, and head south on Route 300. Follow it to its end in Vails Gate (about five miles) at the five-way intersection mentioned above. The Hess station will be on the left. Bear left (not sharp left) onto Route 94 (east). After the next traffic light (Forge Hill Road), the convent will be the first drive on the right. Proceed to the glass-door entrance with a roof overhang. Please park in the area across from the entrance and ring the doorbell to announce your arrival.

If using public transportation, take the Shortline bus from Manhattan (Port Authority bus terminal) to Vails Gate.

History: The Order of St. Helena has always had a close association with the monks of the Order of the Holy Cross. Founded in Kentucky in 1945, the sisters moved their motherhouse in 1952 to "Forge Hill," a former estate on the outskirts of Newburgh, New York.

Description: The guest house, convent, and chapel are attached by a cloister. The newer buildings match the warm red-brick exterior of the former mansion, and all are set in a quiet rural area.

Points of Interest: The Hudson River, Bear Mountain, Washington's last headquarters, and other sights are close to the convent.

Special Note: The sisters welcome individual guests and also sponsor group retreats. Further information may be gotten from the guest sister.

HOLY CROSS MONASTERY
P.O. Box 99
West Park, New York 12493

Telephone: (914) 384–6660.

Order: Order of the Holy Cross (Episcopal).

Accommodations: Up to forty-five guests in the guest house, each with a single room and all with shared bath.

Meals: Three meals daily.

Charges: $40 per day requested to cover the cost of room and meals.

Directions: If driving, take the New York State Thruway to Exit 18 (New Paltz), then take Route 299 east to Route 9W. Go north for four miles; entrance will be on your right.

If using public transportation, from Manhattan take the Metro North train from Grand Central Station to Poughkeepsie or take a bus from the Port Authority bus terminal in Manhattan to New Paltz, New York.

History: Holy Cross Monastery has the distinction of being the oldest monastery in the Episcopal Church. The Reverend James Otis Sargent Huntington founded the order in New York City in 1884. After a couple of moves, he settled the order's motherhouse at West Park in 1904.

Description: The monastery sits on the banks of the Hudson River in the Mid-Hudson Valley. The guest house is the original monastery and is connected with the church and newer monastery. Guests are welcome to join the community in worship and to dine with the monks in their refectory.

Points of Interest: West Park is situated directly across the Hudson River from Hyde Park, where one may visit the Vanderbilt Mansion as well as the Franklin D. Roosevelt home, library, and museum. West Point, historic Newburgh with Washington's last headquarters, and the Huguenot homes in New Paltz are also close by.

Special Note: Holy Cross Monastery welcomes individual guests and also sponsors group retreats. Contact the monastery for information on these.

HOUSE OF THE REDEEMER
7 East 95th Street
New York, New York 10128

Telephone: (212) 289–0399.

Order: (Episcopal).

Accommodations: Fifteen guests in single and twin rooms, some with private baths.

Meals: Meals are provided for those participating in a group retreat. Refrigerator space is available for individual guests to store food.

Charges: Suggested donation of $35 per person per night for room only.

Directions: If driving from Midtown Manhattan, head north on Madison Avenue and then left (west) on East 95th Street.

If using public transportation, take the Madison Avenue bus number M1, M2, M3, or M4 to 95th Street. By subway, take the Lexington Avenue Line #6.

History: The House of the Redeemer is the former Fabbri House. Built between 1914 and 1916, it was the home of Edith Shepard (great-granddaughter of Commodore

Cornelius Vanderbilt) and her husband Ernesto Fabbri. In 1946, Mrs. Fabbri converted her home into a retreat house, thereafter called the House of the Redeemer. It was designated a landmark by the Landmarks Preservation Commission in 1974. Staffed by the Episcopal Community of St. Mary until 1982, the house is now under the stewardship of an independent board of trustees.

Description: Designed by the architect Grosvenor Atterbury, the house was built in the style of an Italian Renaissance palazzo or townhouse. The interior contains many exceptionally fine features, including the library with its woodwork from the fifteenth-century Ducal Palace in Urbino, Italy. Antiques, paintings, and furnishings all combine to make the House of the Redeemer an intact landmark.

Points of Interest: The house is just a few doors away from Manhattan's "museum mile," which runs along Fifth Avenue and the eastern edge of Central Park.

Special Note: For information on group retreats, contact the warden, the Reverend Herbert L. Linley.

LITTLE PORTION FRIARY
St. Joseph's Retreat House
P.O. Box 399
Mt. Sinai, New York 11766

Telephone: (516) 473–0553.

Order: Franciscan brothers (Episcopal).

Accommodations: Sixteen guests in the retreat house. There are ten single rooms, one double, and one quadruple room, all with shared bath.

Meals: Three meals daily.

Charges: $30 to $40 per person per day for room and meals.

Directions: The friary is near the intersection of Routes 25A, 347, and 83, just about in the middle of Long Island. The friars will provide more detailed directions if needed.
   If using public transportation, take the Long Island Railroad from Manhattan (Penn Station). From New England take the ferry (Bridgeport & Port Jefferson

Steamboat Co.) from Bridgeport, Connecticut, to Port Jefferson and arrange in advance for pickup on arrival.

History: This community of Episcopal Franciscan brothers was founded in Wisconsin in 1919 by the Reverend Joseph Crookston. St. Francis and his brethren had a chapel at "Porziuncula," and in 1928 an American "Little Portion" was established on Long Island.

Description: The buildings at Little Portion reflect the simple lifestyle of the brothers. The friary is on more than sixty acres abutting Mt. Sinai Harbor and its wildlife sanctuary.

Points of Interest: Little Portion is in an area that has been designated an historic district.

Special Note: The brothers print a calendar of special programs offered at the friary.

MONASTERY OF MARY THE QUEEN
1310 West Church Street
Elmira, New York 14905

Telephone: Not available.

Order: Dominican nuns (Roman Catholic).

Accommodations: Six women in single rooms. All share bath, kitchenette, and sitting/reading room.

Meals: Meals are self-prepared by guests from supplies provided in the kitchenette.

Charges: $15 per person per day.

Directions: If driving from points east, take Route 17 to the Elmira-Church Street exit. Follow Church Street through the city to the town of Elmira. The monastery is located approximately one mile west of the city line. It is opposite Grandview Avenue and next door to the Elmira Country Club. From points west and south, take Route 390–Route 17 to Exit 48, East Corning. Turn right onto Route 352 to West Water Street and turn left at Grandview Avenue. The monastery is at the end of Grandview Avenue.

If using public transportation, there is plane service to Elmira-Corning Airport. There is also bus service (Greyhound and Trailways) to the terminal on East Church Street in Elmira.

History: The Dominicans trace their history to 1215 when St. Dominic founded the Order of Preachers.

Description: Mary the Queen Retreat Center is surrounded by the beautiful hills of West Elmira.

Special Note: Reservations for retreats should be made one month in advance by writing to the monastery's guest sister, including your name, address, dates requested, and reference (priest or sister). The retreat center is closed during the winter months from November until the end of March. Descriptive literature and map are available on request from the guest sister.

MOUNT SAVIOUR MONASTERY
Pine City, New York 14871

Telephone: (607) 734–1688.

Order: Benedictine monks (Roman Catholic).

Accommodations: Fifteen men in single rooms in St. Joseph's, all with shared bath. In addition, there are accommodations for nine women in single and twin rooms in St. Gertrude's, each with a private bath. In warmer weather, St. Peter's is also open to four guests (women or couples).

Meals: Three meals daily.

Charges: Freewill offering (suggested amount of $20 per night).

Directions: By car, Route 17 is the main highway from both east and west. From the east, take the second Elmira exit, marked "Church Street–Route 352." Follow Church Street through the city to Route 225. Turn left, continue four miles to Mount Saviour Road. From the west, Route 17 passes through Corning. Get into the right lane as you pass Corning Hospital so you can turn right onto Route

225. Be prepared to bear left just after you enter this road. There are two turns, but they are well marked. Continue until you come to Mount Saviour Road.

By public transportation, there are planes to Elmira/Corning Airport (about ten miles away). There is no bus service from the airport to the monastery, so you must take a cab. All out-of-town buses arrive at a common terminal in Elmira. This is also a terminal for local bus service. A local bus marked "Golden Glow" comes to Tolbert's Market, within four miles of the monastery on Route 225. Advance arrangements may be made with the guest master to be picked up at Tolbert's if you will be arriving at the market before 5 p.m. There is no public phone there, so please call the monastery upon arrival at the bus terminal. Do NOT take the bus marked "Pine City."

History: Mount Saviour, named in honor of the Saviour's Transfiguration, was established in 1951 by Father Damasus Winzen and three companions.

Description: Atop Mount Saviour are the monastery's octagonal chapel and towering spire. A fourteenth-century statue of the Virgin stands in the center of the chapel's crypt. Beyond the cluster of the chapel and monastery are over two hundred acres of woodlands and fields.

Points of Interest: The monastery is in the beautiful Finger Lakes region of New York State.

Special Note: Mount Saviour does not accommodate overnight-only guests; the minimum stay is three days with most guests staying three to seven days. Group retreats may be given on special request. A brochure and further information may be gotten from the guest master.

ST. CUTHBERT'S HOUSE AND
ST. AIDAN'S HOUSE
Melrose
R.D. 2
Federal Hill Road
Brewster, New York 10509

Telephone: (914) 278–2610.

Order: Community of the Holy Spirit (Episcopal).

Accommodations: Twenty-four guests in two guest houses in single and twin rooms, all with shared bath.

Meals: Three meals daily.

Charges: $50 per person per night for room and meals.

Directions: If driving from New York City, take the Saw Mill River Parkway or I–87 or I–684 at White Plains. From points west or north, take I–84 or Route 6 (both will bypass Brewster proper to Route 22). Bypassing Brewster,

I–684 becomes Route 22. Proceed as to Pawling. Pass Heidi's Motel on the right and continue about half a mile to a large "New Fairfield" sign on the right up a small incline. Get into the far-right lane. Take Mill Town Road; after about .8 miles, you pass an old cemetery on the left, then go down slight decline, and cross a low bridge. At once the road divides. Do not take the left fork (New Fairfield Road). Take the right fork, Federal Hill Road, .6 miles up the hill to Melrose.

If using public transportation from Manhattan, take Metro North train to Brewster, New York, or bus service to Danbury, Connecticut. From local airports there is limousine service to Danbury, Connecticut.

History: The foundress of the Community of the Holy Spirit was the Reverend Mother Ruth. The child of an interracial marriage, Ruth Elaine Younger joined an Anglican Canadian sisterhood in the 1920s. In 1949, Sr. Ruth returned to her native New York City, there founding a school and, in 1952, the Community of the Holy Spirit. Uncompromising and dynamic, Mother Ruth went on to establish a second school and in 1972 opened St. Cuthbert's Retreat House.

Description: A white clapboard house topped with a Mansard roof, St. Cuthbert's House includes a small chapel, dining room, and a living room area with a fireplace. St. Cuthbert's, St. Aidan's, and the convent are surrounded by 120 acres of woodlands and hills.

Special Note: A full schedule of group retreats is offered at Melrose. A calendar and further information are available from the guest sister.

ST. MARGARET'S HOUSE
Jordan Road
New Hartford, New York 13413

Telephone: (315) 724–2324.

Order: Sisters of St. Margaret (Episcopal).

Accommodations: Sixteen guests (twelve women and four men) in single rooms in the retreat house, all with shared bath.

Meals: Three meals daily.

Charges: $25 per person per day for room and meals.

Directions: If driving on the New York State Thruway, take the New Hartford exit south to Route 8, then right on Route 5 (Genesee Street) and left on Jordan Road.
   If using public transportation, there is plane, train, and bus service to Utica.

History: John Mason Neale, a priest of the Church of England, author, and hymn writer, founded the Society of St. Margaret in 1854. In 1873 three sisters were sent to America to work at Children's Hospital in Boston. The American branch of the society numbers about fifty members today.

Description: St. Margaret's House is set on ten acres of land just south of the city of Utica. The convent and chapel are surroundedd by lawns, trees, and gardens.

Special Note: Group retreats are offered here, and information may be gotten from the guest sister.

ST. MARY'S CONVENT
John Street
Peekskill, New York 10566

Telephone: (914) 737–0113.

Order: Community of St. Mary (Episcopal).

Accommodations: Up to forty guests in St. Benedict's Retreat House and in St. Gabriel's Retreat House. Rooms are single, twin, and (with sofa bed) triple, some with private baths.

Meals: Meals are provided for guests staying in St. Benedict's.

Charges: Suggested contribution of $35 per person per day for room and meals; $25 per day for longer visits.

Directions: If driving, directions and map are available from the convent on request.

   If using public transportation from Manhattan (Grand Central Station), take the train to Peekskill. This will be about an hour's journey. Then take a taxi to the convent, "but depending on time and available cars, sometimes we can meet trains."

History: This, the first religious community in the Episcopal Church, was founded by Harriet Starr Canon and four companions in 1865 in New York City. In 1873 the convent was moved to Peekskill. From the beginning, the community has been involved in a number of works including schools, hospitals, missions, retreat houses, and the making of altar breads.

Description: The convent, built in 1902 of granite quarried on the property, sits on a lovely landscaped setting on the banks of the Hudson River.

Special Note: Contact the guest sister for a brochure and a schedule of group retreats.

TRANSFIGURATION MONASTERY

R.D. 2, Box 2612
Windsor, New York 13865

Telephone: (607) 655–2366.

Order: Camal-
dolese/Benedic-
tine nuns (Roman
Catholic).

Accommodations:
Ten guests in two
guest houses. There
are five single
rooms, two twin,
and one sitting/bedroom, all with shared bath.

Meals: Three meals daily.

Charges: Freewill donations.

Directions: If driving, take Route 17 to Exit 79 (Windsor), then south three and a half miles on Route 79. The monastery will be on the right, just before the golf course.

If using public transportation, there is bus service to Binghamton, New York.

History: Two Benedictine nuns (Sr. Mary Placid Deliard and Sr. Jeanne Marie Pearse) were accepted into the Roman Catholic Diocese of Syracuse in 1975 to establish a Benedictine monastery. Later joined by Sr. Donald Corcoran, the three nuns acquired a suitable property in New York's Southern Tier where they have built their simple and attractive monastery. Recently the community has affiliated with the Camaldolese—a reformed branch of the Benedictine order. Begun by St. Romuald in eleventh-century Italy, Camaldolese monasteries provide for the monastic life-style lived both in community and in hermitages.

Description: Transfiguration Monastery is set on one-hundred acres of woodland and arable river plain nestled at the foot of Horeb Mountain (the "Mountain of God"). Reflecting the nuns' simplicity of spirit and concern for ecology, the monastery is built with natural materials such as wood and stone. Passive solar energy and wood-burning stoves are used.

ST. JOHN'S HOUSE
702 West Cobb Street
Durham, North Carolina 27707

Telephone: (919) 688–4161.

Order: Cowley Fathers (Episcopal).

Accommodations: Three guests in single rooms, all with shared bath.

Meals: Three meals daily.

Charges: The suggested donation is $30 per person per day for room and meals and $75 per weekend (Friday through Sunday afternoon).

Directions: If driving from Greensboro or Henderson, take I–85 to Gregson Street exit, south two miles to Cobb Street. From Chapel Hill take Route 15–501 north to Durham and then Route 15–501 Business three and a half miles to Hill Street at Forest Shopping Center. Turn left on Hill Street to Cobb Street. From Raleigh, take I–40 to the East–West Expressway, then exit at Duke Street.

If using public transportation, there are flights to Raleigh-Durham. Or take a Greyhound/Trailways bus to the La Salle Street Station. Call the house for pickup.

History: The Society of St. John the Evangelist, founded in England in 1866, is the oldest Anglican religious order for men. The Cowley Fathers (as they are commonly called) came to America in 1870, and in 1983 St. John's House was opened as a center for retreats and spiritual direction.

Description: The monastery occupies a house near downtown Durham.

Points of Interest: Duke University and the Duke Forest nature trail are in Durham.

Special Note: St. John's House is closed on Mondays until 6:00 P.M. and during the months of June, July, and August. In order to secure a reservation, each guest is asked to pay a $20 nonrefundable deposit. Group retreats are offered on occasion at the house. A brochure and further information may be gotten from the guest master.

ST. LUKE'S HOUSE
322 East McBee Street
Lincolnton, North Carolina 28092

Telephone: (704) 735–0929.

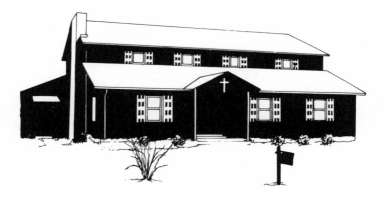

Order: Sisters of the Transfiguration (Episcopal).

Accommodations: Twenty guests in the guest house. There are five rooms with four beds each. All have shared bath.

Meals: Three meals daily.

Charges: Freewill offerings.

Directions: If driving from Charlotte, take Routes 27 and 321 thirty miles northwest. More detailed directions will be provided on request.
   If using public transportation, there is air service to Charlotte. Pickup on arrival can sometimes be arranged.

History: The Sisters of the Transfiguration were founded in 1898. The sisters came to the Episcopal Diocese of

Western North Carolina in 1979 and opened St. Luke's House.

Description: St. Luke's House and St. Luke's Church share the same block of land in the town of Lincolnton.

Special Note: The guest sister can provide information on the house's schedule of retreats and quiet days.

CONVENT OF THE TRANSFIGURATION
495 Albion Avenue
Cincinnati, Ohio 45246

Telephone: (513) 771-5291.

Order: Sisters of the Transfiguration (Episcopal).

Accommodations: Forty-four in the convent and in the guest house. There are thirty single and seven twin rooms, three of which have private baths.

Meals: Three meals daily.

Charges: Freewill offerings accepted.

Directions: If driving from downtown Cincinnati, take I-75 north to Ohio Route 126. Go west on Route 126. At the third light, take a right onto Chester Road, then a left onto Oak Street and right onto Albion Avenue. If coming from the direction of I-275, exit onto I-75 south. Take a right onto Sharon Road, a left at Troy, and a left onto Albion Avenue.

If using public transportation, there is a limousine service ($15) from the airport to Holiday Inn North and the Marriott Inn North on Chester Road. Both inns are near the convent.

History: Eva Lee Matthews (Mother Mary Eva) founded this community in her hometown, the neighborhood of Glendale, Cincinnati, on the Feast of the Transfiguration, 1898. The community's motherhouse remains there to this day.

Description: The convent, guest house, and beautiful chapel of the Transfiguration are all located on the same landscaped property.

Points of Interest: The Taft Museum, Cincinnati Art Museum, and the Mount Airy Arboretum are all in Cincinnati.

Special Note: A brochure and information on group retreats is available from the guest sister.

HOLY PROTECTION MONASTERY
6688 Cady Road
North Royalton, Ohio 44133

Telephone: (216) 237–6800.

Order: Byzantine Poor Clares (Roman Catholic).

Accommodations: Two guests in single rooms in the monastery, both with shared bath.

Meals: Three meals daily.

Charges: No set fee; offerings accepted.

Directions: The guest sister will provide directions on request.

History: St. Francis of Assisi and St. Clare together founded the Poor Clares in 1212. The Monastery of the Holy Protection was opened in 1973.

Description: This is a very small community, unique in that it is the only Poor Clare monastery of the Byzantine Rite Roman Catholics in the United States. The Divine Liturgy and the Divine Office are in English, but of the Byzantine Ruthenian Rite.

Points of Interest: North Royalton is a suburb of Cleveland, known for the Cleveland Art Museum and other places of cultural interest.

MOUNT ANGEL ABBEY RETREAT HOUSE
St. Benedict, Oregon 97373

Telephone: (503) 845–3025.

Order: Benedictine monks (Roman Catholic).

Accommodations: Thirty individual guests (or thirty couples) in thirty rooms, each with a private bath.

Meals: Three meals daily.

Charges: $30 per day per person for room and meals; $52 per day per couple for room and meals.

Directions: By car from Portland, take I–5 south to Woodburn Silverton exit.
   By public transportation from Portland, take train, Greyhound bus, or Hut Airporter south to Woodburn.

History: Mount Angel Abbey traces its roots to the eight-hundred-year-old Abbey of Engelberg, Switzerland. In 1882 a group of monks from Engelberg founded Mount

Angel on top of a hill the Indians had called the "Mount of Communion with God." Though the monastery was twice destroyed by fire (1892 and again in 1926), the monks pressed on and built the present monastery in 1928. The guest house was opened in 1959. The church, library, seminary, and other buildings on the site combine to form an attractive, landscaped setting.

Description: The abbey overlooks the Willamette Valley and enjoys panoramic views—north, east, and south. Visitors are welcome to tour the abbey grounds and to visit the library, abbey museum, and the Russian Center and Museum.

Special Note: The abbey offers group retreats in addition to accommodating individual guests. Brochures are available on request.

EMMAUS
Daylesford Abbey
220 South Valley Road
Paoli, Pennsylvania 19301

Telephone: (215) 647–2530.

Order: Norbertine canons (Roman Catholic).

Accommodations: Four guests in single rooms in Emmaus, all with shared bath.

Meals: Emmaus has a kitchen where guests may prepare their meals.

Charges: Contact the guest master for charges.

Directions: If driving, take the Pennsylvania Turnpike to the Valley Forge exit or take the Schuylkill Expressway to the West Chester exit.
   There is Amtrak train service to Paoli.

History: Norbertines have taught in the Philadelphia area since 1932. Daylesford Priory was opened in 1954 in Paoli, and the present abbey was completed in 1966.

Description: The focal point of the abbey is its large, modern church and adjoining monastery. Emmaus is a small house on the abbey grounds set aside for private retreats and days of recollection.

Points of Interest: Both historic Valley Forge and Philadelphia are within easy reach of the abbey.

Special Note: The abbey's Institute for Religion and Culture offers programs dedicated to religious and cultural renewal. Up to thirty-five participants may stay overnight in single rooms in the monastery. Contact the guest master for a calendar and for further information.

ORTHODOX MONASTERY OF THE TRANSFIGURATION

R.D. 1, Box 184x
Ellwood City, Pennsylvania 16117

Telephone: (412) 758–4002.

Order: Romanian Orthodox nuns (Orthodox Church in America).

Accommodations: Eight guests in four twin rooms in the guest house, all with shared bath.

Meals: Three meals daily.

Charges: Freewill offerings accepted.

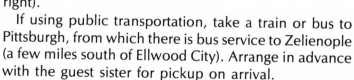

Directions: If driving, take I–79 and exit at exit #28 (Portersville). Then take Route 488 west for six miles to the monastery (on your right).

If using public transportation, take a train or bus to Pittsburgh, from which there is bus service to Zelienople (a few miles south of Ellwood City). Arrange in advance with the guest sister for pickup on arrival.

History: Mother Alexandra, former Princess of Romania, founded the Monastery of the Transfiguration in 1967. The beginnings were humble, the foundress leading a solitary monastic life in a trailer on the one-hundred-acre property. Within a year the trailer was replaced by a redwood building complete with chapel. The sisterhood, which now numbers twelve members, is at an important and exciting chapter in its history. A newer, larger, and more architecturally traditional monastery is under construction.

Description: The new monastery, built around a quadrangle and topped by traditional Romanian-style bell towers, will be set amid the rolling hills of Pennsylvania.

Special Note: After the completion of the building project there will be accommodations for up to twenty guests in single and twin-bedded rooms.

ST. MARGARET'S HOUSE
5419 Germantown Avenue
Philadelphia, Pennsylvania 19144

Telephone: (215) 844–9410.

Order: Sisters of St. Margaret (Episcopal).

Accommodations: Up to eighteen guests in the convent and in the guest house. Three rooms are twin, the others single, and all have shared bath.

Meals: Three meals daily.

Charges: Suggested donation of $25 to $27 per person per day for room and meals.

Directions: If driving, take the New Jersey Turnpike to the Pennsylvania Turnpike. Take Exit 26 (Fort Washington), then Route 309 south to the Mt. Airy exit. Continue straight ahead and then go left onto Germantown Avenue.

Continue on Germantown Avenue for about two miles until you get to St. Luke's Church (on your left). Turn into the driveway; St. Margaret's House is the first building on the left.

If using public transportation, there is Greyhound and Trailways bus service to Philadelphia, as well as Amtrak train service. From downtown Philadelphia at Suburban Station (J.F. Kennedy Boulevard and 16th Street) take the Chestnut Hill Local train to Chelton Avenue Station, Germantown. This will be a seventeen minute ride. Call St. Margaret's House and someone will drive over to pick up.

History: 1989 is the centennial year of the Sisters of St. Margaret in the Episcopal Diocese of Pennsylvania. St. Margaret's House has served the diocese as a retreat and conference center since 1939.

Description: This beautiful stone house was built in 1894. It is on the grounds of the historic St. Luke's Episcopal Church, Germantown.

Points of Interest: Germantown is a part of historic Philadelphia. Independence Hall and other downtown sights are easily accessible by local commuter rail.

Special Note: Individuals and group retreats are welcomed each year from after Labor Day until late June. Further information and schedule of retreats and quiet days may be obtained from the guest sister.

PORTSMOUTH ABBEY
Cory's Lane
Portsmouth, Rhode Island 02871

Telephone: (401) 683–2000.

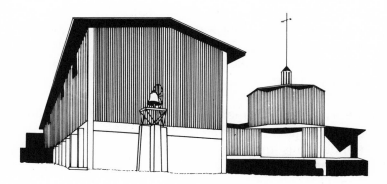

Order: Benedictine monks (Roman Catholic).

Accommodations: Seven men in the monastery in single rooms, two with private baths. There are also accommodations for four women in the manor house in one twin (with private bath) and two single rooms (with shared bath).

Meals: Three meals daily.

Charges: Contact the guest master for information on charges.

Directions: If driving from the greater Boston area, take Route 128 south to Route 24 south. Continue on Route 24 until it merges with and becomes Route 114. Continue south for a short distance; Cory's Lane will be on your right. From Providence, take Route 114 south to Portsmouth. Cory's Lane will be on your right. From the New

York City and southern Connecticut area, take I–95 through Connecticut and pick up Route 138 east in Hope Valley, Rhode Island. Continue east over the Jamestown Bridge to Newport; then take Route 114 north to Portsmouth. As you approach the abbey, there will be a large green sign on the right for "Portsmouth Abbey School." Cory's Lane is just ahead on the left.

If using public transportation from Boston, take a Bonanza bus to the Town Hall, Portsmouth. If traveling from Providence, take a Rhode Island Public Transit bus to Cory's Lane.

History: Leonard Sargent, monk of Downside Abbey and former member of the Episcopal Order of the Holy Cross, founded this monastery of the English Benedictine Congregation in 1918. He was joined by other monks, Dom Hugh Diman among them. Dom Hugh had been an Episcopal deacon and the founder of St. George's School, Middletown, Rhode Island. In 1926 he opened a second prep school at Portsmouth Priory. The priory became an abbey in 1969.

Description: The abbey property, protected by a cross-topped hill on one side and placid Narragansett Bay on the other, includes five hundred acres of woods, farmland, fields, and landscaped campus. Nestled by the bay is the manor house. This summer cottage, an 1860s Upjohn design, housed the original priory. The new monastery and church were completed in 1960.

Points of Interest: The Green Animals Topiary Garden is just across the lane from the abbey, and Newport's mansions and shore are seven miles away.

HOLY SAVIOUR PRIORY

P.O. Box 40
Pineville, South Carolina 29468

Telephone: (803) 351–4356 (call between 8:00 A.M. and 5:00 P.M.).

Order: Order of the Holy Cross (Episcopal).

Accommodations: Twenty-four guests in eight single and sixteen double rooms in the guest house, most with private baths.

Meals: Three meals daily.

Charges: $35 a day or $165 a week per person for room and meals.

Directions: The priory is three miles west of Pineville on South Carolina Route 45, near I–95 and I–26.

If using public transportation, take a plane to Charleston, or Amtrak to Kingstree, or Greyhound bus to St. Stephen. Arrange in advance to be met on arrival.

History: The Order of the Holy Cross was founded by the Reverend James Huntington in 1884.

Description: Situated on several hundred acres of pine forest in the South Carolina Low Country, Holy Saviour Priory includes Marion House (a large plantation house) and a village of one-room hermitages.

Points of Interest: The grave of General Francis Marion (the "Swamp Fox" hero of the American Revolution) is two miles from Marion House and the priory.

Special Note: Contact the priory for brochures and information on its calendar of retreats and day programs.

BLUE CLOUD ABBEY

P.O. Box 98
Marvin, South Dakota 57251

Telephone: (605) 432–5528.

Order: Benedictine monks (Roman Catholic).

Accommodations: Forty guests in the guest wing of the monastery, in twenty twin-bedded rooms, each with a private bath.

Meals: Three meals daily.

Charges: $25 per person per day for room and meals.

Directions: By car, take U.S. Highway 12. The abbey is thirteen miles west of Milbank, South Dakota.
   If using public transportation, take a bus to Milbank or to Watertown, South Dakota.

History: Named for a Native American who had remained faithful to the Church through a period of occasional visits by missionaries, Blue Cloud Abbey was founded in 1954 as a permanent base for ministry among the people of the Dakotas.

Description: The abbey was constructed by the monks themselves and overlooks the vast Whetstone Valley in the Glacial Lakes region of South Dakota.

Points of Interest: Surrounded by many beautiful lakes, the abbey is close to Sisseton/Wahpeton Indian Reservation. Fort Sisseton, dating to the 1860s, is also near the abbey.

Special Note: Both individual guests and retreat groups are welcome at the abbey. Contact the guest master for further information.

WESTON PRIORY
Weston, Vermont 05161

Telephone: (802) 824–5409.

Order: Benedictine monks (Roman Catholic).

Accommodations: Six men in the Priory Guest House, each in a single room and all with shared bath. There are accommodations for five women in Morningside Guest House in two twin and one single room, all with shared bath. (In addition, there are accommodations for a group of up to eight adults in Bethany House and for a group of up to five adults each in Romero House and in Morningside.)

Meals: Individual guests have three meals daily with the brothers. (Groups are requested to bring their own food and to prepare their meals in the kitchen of their guest house.)

Charges: Freewill offering.

Directions: If driving, take I–91 to Exit 6, then Route 103 west to Chester. Continue west on Route 11 and make a right at Hemingway's Motel. When you get to Weston village, make a right onto Route 155 and continue north for four miles. The priory will be on your left.

Contact the guest master for directions by public transportation.

History: A monk of Dormition Abbey in Jerusalem, Abbot Leo Rudloff, founded Weston Priory in 1953.

Description: The simple, rustic monastery, chapel, guest houses, and other buildings are on the edge of the Green Mountain National Forest. The monks of Weston have become widely known for their music and pottery. Albums, cassettes, songbooks, and crafts are sold at the priory.

Points of Interest: Often called the prettiest village in Vermont, Weston is on the National Register of Historic Places. The Weston Playhouse is the oldest professional summer theatre in Vermont. The Old Parish Church (1803) and the Church on the Hill are fine examples of nineteenth-century rural New England ecclesiastical architecture.

Special Note: The ordinary length of stay at the priory guest houses is from three days to one week. Reservations should be made at least four months in advance. Maps, brochures, and further information are available from the priory's guest master.

MONASTERY OF THE VISITATION

Monte Maria
Route 1, Box 2055
Rockville, Virginia 23146

Telephone: (804) 749–4885.

Order: Visitation nuns (Roman Catholic).

Accommodations: Two women in the monastery, each in a single room and both with shared bath.

Meals: Three meals daily.

Charges: Donation.

Directions: If driving, contact the guest sister for directions.
   There is bus, train, and air service to Richmond, Virginia. Arrange in advance with the guest sister to be met on arrival.

History: The Visitation nuns are an order of cloistered, contemplative women founded in 1610 by St. Francis de Sales and St. Frances de Chantel. The Monastery of the Visitation was founded in Richmond, Virginia, in the

1860s and remained there for about 120 years. The community moved to its new home in Rockville in April 1987.

Description: The monastery has 156 acres of beautiful rolling Virginia farmland.

Special Note: Women who wish to have more information about retreats at Monte Maria should contact Mother Margaret Mary McGuire.

CONVENT OF ST. HELENA
1114 21st Avenue East
Seattle, Washington 98112–3513

Telephone: (206) 325–2830.

Order: Order of St. Helena
(Episcopal).

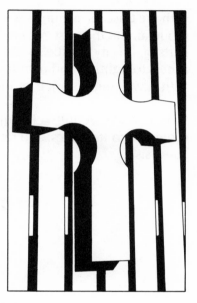

Accommodations: Eight
guests in the convent in
four twin-bedded rooms,
all with shared bath.

Meals: Three meals daily.

Charges: Freewill offerings
accepted, but $25 per day
per person for room and
meals is suggested.

Directions: If driving, exit
from I–5 onto East Madi-
son Street, going east.
Turn left onto 19th Avenue East. Pass two four-way stop
signs with red blinkers. At the next street, turn right (east)
on East Prospect Street, then left onto 21st Avenue East.
The convent is the second house on the right.

If using public transportation from downtown Seattle,
take Metro bus 12, labeled for Interlaken Park. (This bus
can be boarded at 1st Avenue at Union or on Marion
Street.) Get off at 19th Avenue East and East Prospect
Street. Walk two blocks east to 21st Avenue East. Turn
left. The convent is the second house on the right.

History: This, the newest foundation of the Order of St.
Helena, was opened in 1983.

Description: The convent is a large private house in the Capital Hill district of Seattle. Built about 1910, the house is "Seattle Tudor" in style and is built in a residential area of similar homes.

Points of Interest: Seattle is located on the Puget Sound, with the Cascade Mountains to the east and the Olympic Mountains to the west. Mount Ranier is visible from many parts of the city. Seattle's Metro bus system provides easy access to sights in and near the city. There are two parks within walking distance of the convent.

Special Note: A full schedule of events (quiet days/ evenings, conferences, and retreats) is available from the guest sister.

ST. MARTIN'S ABBEY GUEST HOUSE
Lacey, Washington 98503

Telephone: (206) 438–4457.

Order: Benedictine monks (Roman Catholic).

Accommodations: Eighteen guests in ten rooms (two single and eight twin). Each room has a sink and shared bath down the corridor.

Meals: Three meals daily.

Charges: $20 per person per day for room and meals.

Directions: By car from Seattle, take I–5 about sixty miles south to Lacey.
   There is air service to Seattle-Tacoma Airport (about one hour north of Lacey). Amtrak and Greyhound have service to Olympia (about two miles south of Lacey).

History: When Benedictine monks arrived in Washington in 1895, the Pacific Northwest was still a pioneer region.

From its inception, education was a priority at St. Martin's, and today these monks administer and teach at the coeducational St. Martin's College.

Description: The guest house and campus share an attractive, peaceful, and tranquil setting. The abbey church was completed in 1972. Its warm wooden interior, rich with symbolism and art, is designed for a flexible use of space and has become the model for a number of churches of various denominations.

Points of Interest: The Pacific Northwest is heavily wooded with tall fir, cedar, hemlock, and other species of trees. The Pacific Ocean is a forty-five minute drive west of the abbey, and the historic sights of Seattle are one hour's drive north. The majestic Mount Ranier can be seen for many miles and from many directions.

Special Note: A brochure describing the guest house is available from the abbey's guest master. Groups are welcome at the abbey but must provide their own retreat director.

CONVENT OF THE HOLY NATIVITY
101 East Division Street
Fond du Lac, Wisconsin 54935

Telephone: (414) 921–2560.

Order: Sisters of the Holy Nativity (Episcopal).

Accommodations: Twenty-seven guests in the convent in single rooms, all with shared bath.

Meals: Three meals daily.

Charges: $20 per person per day for room and meals.

Directions: Contact the convent's guest sister for directions.

History: The Sisterhood of the Holy Nativity was begun in Boston in 1882 by Charles Chapman Grafton, a priest of the Episcopal Church. When consecrated bishop of Fond du Lac, the sisters followed Bishop Grafton to Wisconsin, there establishing the Convent of the Holy Nativity.

Description: The Gothic Revival convent, built at the turn of the century, has an exceptionally beautiful chapel, its interior fitted with fine wood carving. In the spirit of the founder, the sisters "open their chapels generously for retreats and private devotions of the devout-minded, whether Associates of the Sisterhood or not."

Points of Interest: Fond du Lac has long been a center for the Anglo-Catholic movement in the Episcopal Church. The city's Cathedral Church of St. Paul is listed on the National Register of Historic Places.

Special Note: Group retreats are offered several times a year at the convent. Descriptive brochures and further information may be obtained from the convent's guest sister.

DE KOVEN CENTER

600 21st Street
Racine, Wisconsin 53403

Telephone: (414) 633–1650.

Order: Order of Julian of Norwich (Episcopal).

Accommodations: Thirty-two guests in twin-bedded rooms, all with shared bath.

Meals: Three meals daily.

Charges: $10 per person per night; freewill offering accepted for meals.

Directions: If driving, take I–94 to Route 11 east to Route 32 north. Turn left on 21st Street to the center.
  If using public transportation, there is air service to Milwaukee International Airport and train service to Sturtevant, Wisconsin.

History: A priest of the Episcopal Church, Fr. John-Julian began this Anglican contemplative community in Norwich, Connecticut, in 1982. The order's namesake and patroness is Dame Julian of Norwich, the fourteenth-century English mystic and anchoress. Patterned on medieval religious orders such as the English Gilbertines, the order has both monks and nuns, all of whom have equal status. In 1988 the members moved west to staff the De Koven Center, a conference and retreat center of the Episcopal Diocese of Milwaukee.

Description: The center is on beautifully landscaped property on the shore of Lake Michigan. Built as a college between 1854 and 1874, the buildings are Gothic Revival in style.

Points of Interest: Frank Lloyd Wright's Johnson's Wax Building is close by, as is the largest marina on the Great Lakes.

Special Note: A calendar of the center's group retreats and conferences is available on request.

ST. NORBERT ABBEY
De Pere, Wisconsin 54115–2697

Telephone: (414) 336–2727.

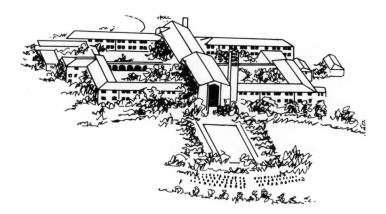

Order: Norbertine canons (Roman Catholic).

Accommodations: Sixty guests in single rooms, each room with its own sink. All have shared bath.

Meals: Three meals daily.

Charges: Rooms are $15.50 per person per night; breakfast is $3.25; lunch is $3.50; and dinner is $5.50.

Directions: From I–43, exit at signs for the airport and Highway 172 (Exit 108). Take this to the exit for Webster Avenue and turn left (south). Go approximately one and a quarter miles to the abbey—on the right (west) side of the road. From Highway 41, take the first exit north of De Pere exit (labeled Highway 172 and Austin Straubel Airport). Stay on the right—take Highway 172 over the river and take the first exit for Webster Avenue. Turn right (south) and go one and a quarter miles. The abbey will be on the right (west) side of the road.

There is plane and bus service to Green Bay. The abbey is only fifteen minutes away by taxi.

History: St. Norbert founded this Order of Canons Regular in Premontre, France, in 1120. The canons arrived in Wisconsin in 1893 to minister to Dutch, Belgian, and French immigrants, and in 1925 St. Norbert Abbey was established in De Pere.

Description: The abbey is set on 160 acres in an urban setting. Guests are invited to join the canons in the Norbertine community liturgies—morning praise, evensong, and the eucharist.

Points of Interest: The Heritage Hill State Park is one mile from the abbey, and the Door County Peninsula Resort Area is about a one-and-a-half hour drive away.

Special Note: Contact the guest master for information about group retreats.